Dream Catchers
Teacher's Guide

Third Edition

Developing Career and Educational Awareness

Norene Lindsay

America's Career Publisher

Dream Catchers Teacher's Guide, *Third Edition*

Developing Career and Educational Awareness

© 2004 by JIST Publishing, Inc.

Published by JIST Works, an imprint of JIST Publishing, Inc.
8902 Otis Avenue
Indianapolis, IN 46216-1033

Phone: 800-648-JIST   Fax: 800-JIST-FAX
E-mail: info@jist.com   Web site: www.jist.com

> **Note to instructors.** *Dream Catchers Teacher's Guide,* Third Edition, is part of a complete curriculum that includes a student workbook, this teacher's guide, and a book of reproducible activities. All materials are available separately from JIST.
>
> **Videos and other materials** on career exploration are also available from JIST. A CD-ROM and Web site with information on over 14,000 jobs is available through CareerOINK.com. The Web site offers information at free and subscription levels. Call 1-800-648-JIST for details.
>
> **Quantity discounts are available for JIST products.** Please call 1-800-648-JIST or visit www.jist.com for a free catalog and more information.
>
> **Visit www.jist.com.** Find out about our products, order a catalog, and link to other career-related sites. You can also learn more about JIST authors and JIST training available to professionals.

Acquisitions Editor: Randy Haubner
Development Editor: Veda Dickerson
Cover and Interior Designer: Aleata Howard
Interior Layout: Carolyn J. Newland
Proofreaders: Jeanne Clark, David Faust

Printed in the United States of America

07 06 05 04 03   9 8 7 6 5 4 3 2 1

All rights reserved. No part of this book may be reproduced in any form or by any means, or stored in a database or retrieval system, without prior permission of the publisher except in the case of brief quotations embodied in articles or reviews. Making copies of any part of this book for any purpose other than your own personal use is a violation of United States copyright laws.

We have been careful to provide accurate information throughout this book, but it is possible that errors and omissions have been introduced. Please consider this in making any career plans or other important decisions. Trust your own judgment above all else and in all things.

Trademarks: All brand names and product names used in this book are trade names, service marks, trademarks, or registered trademarks of their respective owners.

ISBN 1-59357-004-X

About This Book

Dream Catchers Teacher's Guide provides tips, techniques, and specific activities for structuring a career awareness program. It is designed to support the student workbook titled *Dream Catchers: Developing Career and Educational Awareness,* and is most effective when also used in conjunction with *Dream Catchers Activities*, a collection of reproducible activity sheets.

A great advantage of this book and the other *Dream Catchers* materials is that they can also be used in virtually any course to supplement that material. Activities can be presented in the order in which they appear in the student workbook. They can also be rearranged in any order your choose.

Dream Catchers Teacher's Guide follows the structure of the student workbook and then adds one additional part. Parts 1, 2, and 3 of the Teacher's Guide correspond to the same three parts in *Dream Catchers*. Part 4 of this guide provides activities and suggestions for creating your own unit on the relationship between work and the needs and functions of society.

Table of Contents

Introduction 1

Lesson Plans for Part 1
Capture Your Dreams—The Choice Is Yours   7

    Introducing the *Dream Catchers* Concept and the Workbook 8
    What Is a Cluster? 9
    Discovering Career Clusters 10
    Find the Right Career Cluster 10
    Discovering Data, People, and Things 12
    Working with Data 13
    Working with People 15
    Working with Things and Machinery 16
    Discovering Working Conditions 17
    Who Will You Work For? 19
    The Freedom to Choose 20
    Discovering Careers 21
    Career Data Worksheet 21
    Some Careers to Research 21
    Another Kind of Work 23
    Running a Home Is a Big Job! 25
    Capture Your Dreams 26

Lesson Plans for Part 2
The Stuff Dreams Are Made Of—Discovering Your Skills   27

    What Are Skills? 28
    Academic Skills Are Building Blocks 29
    Building a Skills Tower 31
    How Strong Is Your Tower? 31
    Do Workers Need Academic Skills? 33
    What Are Self-Management Skills? 34
    My Good Self-Management Skills 35
    Do Employees Get Report Cards? 36

What Are Job-Related Skills? 37
    Where Can You Learn Job-Related Skills? 38
    Mapping Your Future 38
    How Is School Like a Job? 39
    The Stuff Dreams Are Made Of 40

Lesson Plans for Part 3
Making Dreams Come True—Ability, Effort, and Achievement   41
    A Modern Fable of *The Three Little Pigs* 42
    Ability, Effort, and Achievement 43
    Know Your Strengths. 44
    . . . And Weaknesses 44
    Turning a Weakness into a Strength 45
    You Can Improve, Too! 46
    Managing Your Study Time 47
    A Time-Management Quiz 49
    Organizing Your Workplace at Home 50
    My Workplace Plan 51
    Setting Achievement Goals 53
    Make Dreams Come True 55

Lesson Plans for Part 4
Putting Your Dreams to Work—Work and the Needs and Functions of Society   57
    What You Need to Know About Part 4 58
    Why Do People Work? 59
    Job Satisfaction—What Do You Want? 60
    Why Do You Work? 61
    Work and Society 62
    Changes in Society and Work 63
    The Changing Workforce—Jobs for Robots 64
    What Would Happen If. 65
    On Strike! 66
    What Are Goods and Services? 67
    Services for Your Home 68
    Where Do Goods Come From? 69
    The Global Economy 70
    Goods from Around the World 71

Appendix—Answer Key   73

Notes   78

Introduction

What You Need to Know About the *Dream Catchers* Curriculum Materials

This is an introduction to the many facets and features of the *Dream Catchers* materials for developing career and educational awareness in the intermediate grades. Completing *Dream Catchers* can be a fun and rewarding experience for you and your students. Here's some information you will need to know.

Why the *Dream Catchers* Materials Were Written

It's no secret that our entire educational system has come under intense scrutiny, and that scrutiny is not likely to diminish in the near future. One of our nation's primary concerns is whether or not we will continue to produce a quality workforce in the 21st century.

By and large, society charges educators with the responsibility of producing quality workers. But changes in the worldwide economy, technology, the nature of work, and attitudes of employers and workers have occurred at such a rapid pace that teachers have a difficult time taking them all in. However, as an educator, you are expected to respond to those changes and prepare your students for the future.

One response to this challenge has been a growing movement across the country to include career awareness and exploration as an integral part of the school curriculum. Instruction starts in kindergarten. Few people would quarrel with the philosophy behind this movement, yet practical concerns do exist.

Educators and counselors already have full agendas trying to improve academic achievement. Adding another subject area takes time, planning, and increased expertise. This is especially true in the elementary and intermediate grades where counselors can be few in number and overburdened. The role of career educator, therefore, frequently falls on the classroom teacher.

Dream Catchers materials were written because we recognize the need for standardized, comprehensive career education in the intermediate grades. We also recognize the educator's need for career awareness materials that can be

Dream Catchers Teacher's Guide

easily integrated into the curriculum. We've done the research. We've provided the activities. We've prepared the lesson plans. We truly believe this book is *your* dream come true!

Dream Catchers Materials Are Easy to Use

Your needs and the needs of your students were foremost in our plans when developing these books. When you read about the design features below, you'll see why we make this claim with confidence.

Backed by Solid Research

Recognizing the need for standardized and comprehensive materials, we turned to the experts for our research—the National Career Development Guidelines.

The guidelines contain specific competencies and indicators for developing career information. The competencies represent broad goals, and the indicators represent specific knowledge, skills, and abilities to achieve those goals. The *Dream Catchers* materials are based on and fulfill the competencies related to self-knowledge, educational and occupational exploration, and career planning.

Organized into Three Parts

The *Dream Catchers* student workbook is organized into three parts, each focusing on a separate topic. Although all topics are logically linked, each part is designed as a separate entity, independent of the other parts. This design allows you to use the book in any order and to use the separate parts at different times of the year. Of course, it also can be used from start to finish as a complete unit.

Part 1: Capture Your Dreams—The Choice Is Yours

The first part develops an awareness of the world of work by providing skills for understanding and using career information. Students learn they can make choices based on career clusters and work conditions. They discover the difference between working for others and being self-employed, and they explore the changing roles of women and men in the workplace. The importance of volunteer work and the work involved in running a home are also covered.

Part 2: The Stuff Dreams Are Made Of—Discovering Your Skills

This part develops an awareness of the relationship between schoolwork and the world of work. Students examine the skills (including SCANS skills) needed at school and on the job. Featured are academic skills, self-management skills, and job-related skills. Students also learn about the variety of educational and training options to obtain job-related skills.

Part 3: Make Dreams Come True—Ability, Effort, and Achievement

This part concentrates on how ability, effort, and achievement affect a student's success in school and at work. It provides students with the tools needed to identify their strengths and weaknesses in both academic and self-management areas. It provides methods to change weaknesses into strengths. Students are guided in setting goals and implementing a personal plan of action for meeting their goals.

Teacher's Guide Has Additional Part

You will note that the student workbook has three parts, while the teacher's guide and the activities book each have four. This final part is titled "Putting Your Dreams to Work—Work and the Needs and Functions of Society." It provides extra material that is not included in the student workbook. It describes the relationship between people's jobs and various aspects of the world of work.

The following chart provides a comparison of the parts pages in the three *Dream Catchers* books.

	Student Workbook	Teacher's Guide	Activities Book
Part 1	Pages 1–30	Pages 7–26	Pages 3–51
Part 2	Pages 31–52	Pages 27–40	Pages 52–77
Part 3	Pages 53–70	Pages 41–56	Pages 78–102
Part 4	N/A	Pages 57–72	Pages 103–118

Designed for Maximum Flexibility

You can easily adapt the *Dream Catchers* books for use in a variety of settings. This *Dream Catchers Teacher's Guide* contains a good mix of individual, small group, and class activities. Students can complete many of the activities on

Dream Catchers Teacher's Guide

their own or guided by a teacher. This mix ensures the *Dream Catchers* materials will work with a variety of student populations, including students who are at-risk and those with special needs.

The optional *Dream Catchers Activities* book is a real bonus. It contains over 80 reproducible activity sheets that correspond to the activities in the *Dream Catchers* workbook and in this *Dream Catchers Teacher's Guide.* It and this teacher's guide contain a series of worksheets that make up Part 4. The topic of Part 4 is "Work and the Needs and Functions of Society." The reproducible worksheets enable you to expand and enhance any concept in the *Dream Catchers* workbook. Again, these activities contain a mix of individual, small-group, and whole-class activities that can be used in class or as homework.

Many of the activities in the *Dream Catchers* books encourage parental and community involvement. Students write letters, interview, study local businesses, read the want ads, and perform many other activities that take them beyond the school walls.

Requires No Training to Use

Dream Catchers Teacher's Guide provides complete lesson plans for each activity in the workbook and on the reproducible activity sheets. You don't have to research or plan a thing because it's been done for you. Below is a sample lesson plan page from this *Teacher's Guide.* The key to the sample is on page 5.

Sample Teacher's Guide Lesson Plan

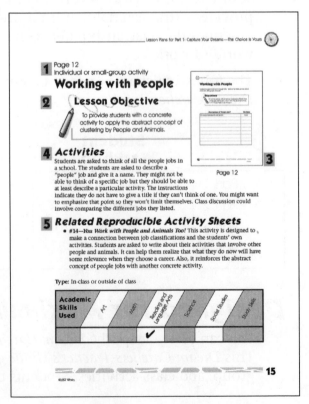

©JIST Works

Key to Sample Teacher's Guide Lesson Plan Page

1 The first section of each lesson plan gives the title of the activity. This title will match the title of the activity in the workbook. The text above the title tells you what page the corresponding activity is on in the student workbook. Another line indicates how the activity can be used.

- **Individual** refers to activities the students can work on independently.
- **Small group** designates activities that are suitable for use in a small group.
- **Class** indicates activities that can be completed by the whole class as a group.

2 The next section of the lesson plan includes the "Lesson Objective," which states the purpose of the lesson in one or two sentences.

3 Beside the lesson objective is a picture of the corresponding page in the student workbook and a reminder of the workbook page number.

4 The "Activities" section explains what the students are asked to do. It suggests points you might like to highlight before students begin the activity. It also provides discussion topics and other ideas for further developing the objective.

5 "Related Reproducible Activity Sheets" lists activities from *Dream Catchers Activities* that you can use in conjunction with this activity. Some *Dream Catchers* activities do not have related reproducible activity sheets and others will have more than one. Some activity sheets are shown. This section tells you

- How the reproducible activity sheets can be used—as class activities or as homework activities
- The number and title of the reproducible activity sheet
- The purpose and content of the activity
- A chart of academic skills with check marks that indicate which skills the activity develops

Lesson Plans for — **Part 1**

Capture Your Dreams— The Choice Is Yours

Pages iii and vi
Class activity

Introducing the *Dream Catchers* Concept and the Workbook

Lesson Objective

To introduce the new unit of study on developing career and educational awareness.

Activities

To introduce this unit, you might want to read "About This Book" and "What Is a Dream Catcher" to the class from the workbook. The driving concept behind this book is that students will have many choices to make in the future, and the *Dream Catchers* materials will help them make the choices that are right for them. Stress that knowledge will give them the power to shape their futures and make their "dreams come true."

Related Reproducible Activity Sheets

- **#1—*Write a Letter Home.*** This activity gives students step-by-step instructions on writing a letter home explaining *Dream Catchers*.

- **#2—*Make Your Own Dream Catcher.*** This activity gives instructions on how to make an actual dream catcher. The instructions cover making a dream catcher about 11 inches in circumference. However, dream catchers can be made in any size with any materials that will work for the frame. Small dream catchers can be made using pipe cleaners for the frame.

Type: In-class

Academic Skills Used	Art	Math	Reading and Language Arts	Science	Social Studies	Study Skills
	✓		✓			

Page 2
Individual or small-group activity

What Is a Cluster?

Lesson Objective

To introduce students to the concept of clustering or categorizing things by their similarities.

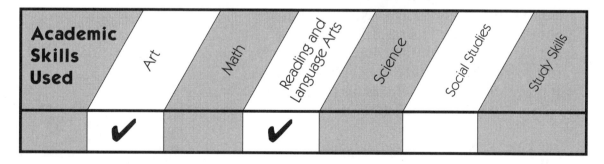

Page 2

Activities

This activity is used as a warm up to introduce the concept of career clusters, which follows. Students are asked to assign names to clusters of things. The clusters have been designed so students may think of different names for the same cluster. For example, the cluster "dog, cat, hamster, goldfish, bird" might elicit differing cluster names such as "animals" or "pets." Through class discussion, guide students to realize that the more specific the cluster name, the better.

Related Reproducible Activity Sheets

- **#3—*Make Your Own Cluster Games.*** The activity sheet provides more experiences with clustering through game formats.

Type: In-class or outside of class

Academic Skills Used	Art	Math	Reading and Language Arts	Science	Social Studies	Study Skills
	✔		✔			

Pages 3–7
Individual or small-group activity

Discovering Career Clusters

Pages 8–9
Individual or small-group activity

Find the Right Career Cluster

Lesson Objective

To introduce students to the concept of career clusters as one method of exploring careers that may interest them. Students are asked to apply their new knowledge.

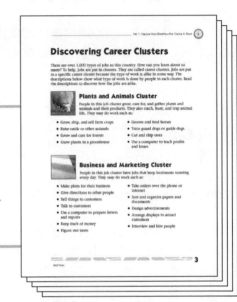

Pages 3–7

Activities

Although a variety of clustering taxonomies exist for jobs, the nine used in "Discovering Career Clusters" (pages 3–7) were selected because they are more concrete and, therefore, more understandable for students this age. Students can read the descriptions themselves, or you can read them together as a class. The activity, "Find the Right Career Cluster" (pages 8–9), asks students to select the cluster definition which matches the career pictured. Make sure to tell students they will probably need to refer back to the definitions on pages 3–7 to do the matching.

"Checking" their answers can be done through small group comparison/corrections or through class discussion. Further activities might include discussing which clusters sound appealing to various students and seeing if they can think of other jobs in each cluster.

Pages 8–9

Lesson Plans for Part 1: Capture Your Dreams—The Choice Is Yours

Related Reproducible Activity Sheets

- **#4—*Career Cluster Collages.*** Students can further explore the concept of career clusters by making career cluster collages.

- **#5–13—*Career Cluster Worksheets*** (one for each cluster). Also, an activity sheet is available for each cluster that contains the cluster definition. These can be used for brainstorming occupations in a cluster, and they are also used with two other activities: *Career Cluster Collages* (Activity #4) and *Make a Career Cluster Handbook* (Activity #23).

Type: In-class or outside of class

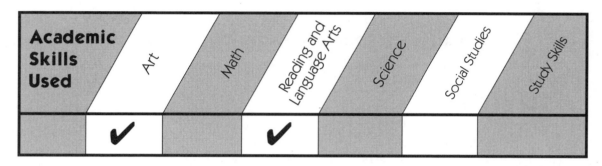

Academic Skills Used	Art	Math	Reading and Language Arts	Science	Social Studies	Study Skills
	✔		✔			

Dream Catchers Teacher's Guide

Page 10
Individual or class activity

Discovering Data, People, and Things

Lesson Objective

To introduce students to the concept of "Data, People, and Things" as another method of clustering careers and exploring careers that may interest them.

Page 10

Activities

Students may simply read the definitions on this page individually and proceed to the next three activities. These activities ask them to apply their new knowledge of "Data, People, and Things" through writing about each. As a class activity, the definitions could be read out loud. Sample jobs are provided. Each definition and discussion could elicit more jobs that would fit in each category.

Jobs, of course, are rarely classified as only "Data, People, or Things." That's why the definition of this clustering says, "who or what people work with *most* of the time." You can judge by the age level or sophistication of your class as to whether or not you want to introduce the concept of multiple classifications. You may want to introduce this concept after they have completed the activities asking them to apply their new knowledge. For example, a teacher is primarily a people job, yet a teacher also has to work with data—that is, papers, grades, and so forth.

Lesson Plans for Part 1: Capture Your Dreams—The Choice Is Yours

Page 11
Individual or small-group activity

Working with Data

Lesson Objective

To provide students with a concrete activity to apply the abstract concept of clustering by Data.

Page 11

Activities

Students are asked to think about what kind of data would be gathered by a meteorologist. Data is certainly the most abstract concept of the "Data, People, and Things" classification and will, perhaps, be the most difficult for students to fully grasp. That's why this activity centers on a specific job and the data involved with that job. Because our objective is simply to introduce students to the "data" concept, you can decide by the level of your class how thoroughly you wish to explore this classification.

The definition does list a variety of jobs that are primarily classified as data jobs. You may want to have class discussion as to what kind of data people working at those jobs would gather and what they would do with it.

Related Reproducible Activity Sheets

- **#16—*You Work with Data Too!*** This activity is designed to make a connection between job classifications and the students' own activities. Students are asked to write about their activities that involve using data. It can help them realize that what they do now will have some relevance when they choose a career. Also, it reinforces the abstract concept of data jobs with another concrete activity.

- Although "data" is the most abstract concept, students are involved in a lot of data activities. Certainly schoolwork would fall under that category. Also, any hobbies or collecting (baseball cards, sports statistics, keeping track of a paper route, etc.) would also be data work. On the creative "ideas" part of data, artwork and dramatics would apply.

Type: In-class or outside of class

Academic Skills Used	Art	Math	Reading and Language Arts	Science	Social Studies	Study Skills
			✓			

Lesson Plans for Part 1: Capture Your Dreams—The Choice Is Yours

Page 12
Individual or small-group activity

Working with People

Lesson Objective

To provide students with a concrete activity to apply the abstract concept of clustering by People and Animals.

Page 12

Activities

Students are asked to think of all the people jobs in a school. The students are asked to describe a "people" job and give it a name. They might not be able to think of a specific job but they should be able to at least describe a particular activity. The instructions indicate they do not have to give a title if they can't think of one. You might want to emphasize that point so they won't limit themselves. Class discussion could involve comparing the different jobs they listed.

Related Reproducible Activity Sheets

- **#14—*You Work with People and Animals Too!*** This activity is designed to make a connection between job classifications and the students' own activities. Students are asked to write about their activities that involve other people and animals. It can help them realize that what they do now will have some relevance when they choose a career. Also, it reinforces the abstract concept of people jobs with another concrete activity.

Type: In-class or outside of class

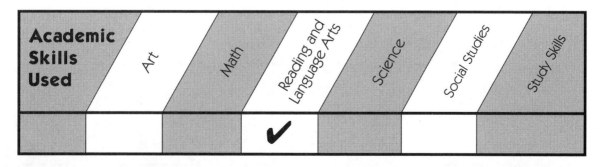

Dream Catchers Teacher's Guide

Page 13
Individual or small-group activity

Working with Things and Machinery

Lesson Objective

To provide students with a concrete activity to apply the abstract concept of clustering by Things and Machinery.

Page 13

Activities

Students are asked to think of all the things and machinery jobs that are necessary to turn a tree into a table.

This activity is set up in columns where they describe the job and give it a name. It might be more difficult to think of an actual job title with this category, but they should be able to at least describe a particular activity. Again, emphasize they do not have to give a title so they won't limit themselves. Encourage them to really concentrate on all the "steps" necessary to produce a table from a tree. Class discussion could involve comparing the different jobs they listed.

Related Reproducible Activity Sheets

- **#15—*You Work with Things and Machinery Too!*** This activity is designed to make a connection between job classifications and the students' own activities. Students are asked to write about their activities that involve things and machinery. It can help them realize that what they do now will have some relevance when they choose a career. Also, it reinforces the abstract concept of things and machinery jobs with another concrete activity. Considering all the "technological toys" they play with (which certainly come under the heading of "things") and all household "gadgets," they should be able to think of long lists for this activity.

Type: In-class or outside of class

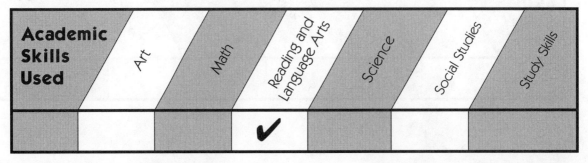

Academic Skills Used	Art	Math	Reading and Language Arts	Science	Social Studies	Study Skills
			✔			

©JIST Works

Lesson Plans for Part 1: Capture Your Dreams—The Choice Is Yours

Page 14
Individual activity

Discovering Working Conditions

Lesson Objective

To introduce students to the concept of Working Conditions as another way to cluster and explore careers that might interest them.

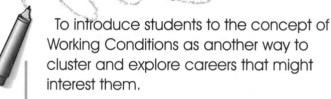

Page 14

Activities

Students are first asked to think of things they do inside and outside as a way of introducing the concept of "Working Conditions." The most basic working conditions, "Inside" and "Outside," are defined for them, and they are asked to match the definition with a job. They need to carefully read the definition of "Inside" to be able to correctly classify the jobs listed. For example, an airplane obviously flies outside, but the pilot has an "Inside" job.

Class discussion might involve seeing how many students have parent(s) or guardians who work inside or outside. You might also ask them to list other jobs that can be classified as "Inside" or "Outside."

Related Reproducible Activity Sheets

- **#17—*Discovering More Working Conditions*.** If you desire to introduce students to more working conditions, this activity sheet defines four more: Both Inside and Out, Noise Level, Temperature, and Safety. You can discuss the fact that one job can have multiple working condition classifications if you choose—that is, a window washer has an outside job with safety factors. The activity asks them to list jobs under each category, and it is a good exercise for small group competition.

Dream Catchers Teacher's Guide

Type: In-class or outside of class

Academic Skills Used	Art	Math	Reading and Language Arts	Science	Social Studies	Study Skills
			✔			

Lesson Plans for Part 1: Capture Your Dreams—The Choice Is Yours

Pages 16–17
Individual activity

Who Will You Work For?

Lesson Objective

To introduce students to the concept that some people in the workforce work for others (employees), and some people work for themselves (self-employed).

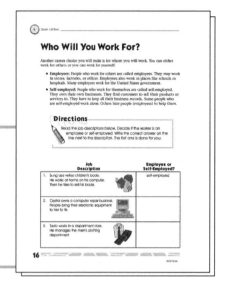

Pages 16–17

Activities

Students are given the definitions of "employees" and "self-employed" and are asked to apply those definitions to job descriptions. Answers can be checked by comparing and correcting answers in small groups or through class discussion.

Related Reproducible Activity Sheets

- **#18—*Conduct a Workforce Survey.*** This activity further explores the idea of who people work for by asking students to gather data on employees and self-employed people and analyze the results.

- **#19—*Learning About Self-Employment.*** This activity sheet explores self-employment by having the student interview a self-employed person. The interview information is then written as a report.

Type: In-class or outside of class

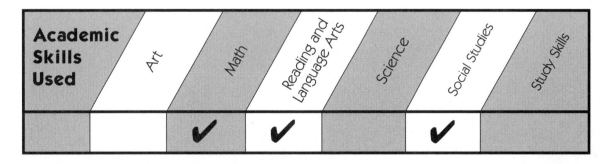

Academic Skills Used	Art	Math	Reading and Language Arts	Science	Social Studies	Study Skills
		✔	✔		✔	

Pages 18–19
Individual or small-group activity

The Freedom to Choose

Lesson Objective

To encourage students to think of careers in terms of skills, interests, and abilities rather than gender stereotypes.

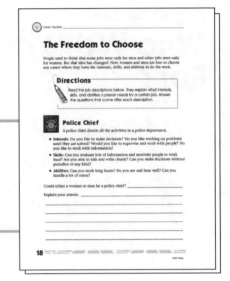

Pages 18–19

Activities

Students are asked to read job descriptions for a Police Chief and a Registered Nurse. Then they are asked to consider if either a woman or a man could perform these jobs. Of course, these two jobs are chosen because people do have gender stereotypes concerning them.

Class discussion on this topic could center on first defining what a stereotype is, and then why we stereotype certain jobs by gender. You might ask students to list jobs they think of as "men's work" and "women's work." Then ask them to think of the skills, abilities, and interests necessary to perform those jobs. Next they can explore whether or not these jobs could be held by either a man or a woman.

Further discussion might involve jobs where gender stereotyping has been "broken," for example, women in construction. You might even have them consider why women have moved into "men's" jobs more readily than men have moved into "women's" jobs. They might also consider if there are any jobs that are mostly for "women only" or "men only." (Professional sports usually come up here, so be ready for it!) These topics can elicit some pretty lively class discussion.

Lesson Plans for Part 1: Capture Your Dreams—The Choice Is Yours

Page 20
Individual activity

Discovering Careers

Pages 21–22
Individual activity

Career Data Worksheet

Pages 23–24
Individual activity

Some Careers to Research

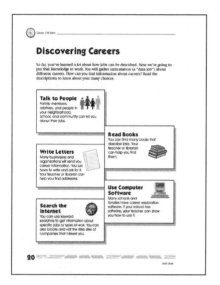

Page 20

Pages 21–22

Pages 23–24

Lesson Objective

To introduce students to career exploration and research and allow them to perform some research activities.

Activities

"Discovering Careers" on page 20 introduces students to the various methods available to learn about specific careers: interviews, books, letters, software, and the Internet. If you want to have your students write letters for career information, the best source of current addresses is the *Occupational Outlook Handbook.* The *Handbook* should be available in most libraries and can also be ordered from JIST Works.
(Call 1-800-648-JIST for ordering information.)

©JIST Works

A good method to begin career research is to allow the students to interview you and fill out pages 21–22, the "Career Data Worksheet." This worksheet is also available as a reproducible activity sheet, so if you want your students to do more research, you can duplicate copies for them to use. Interviewing is a good technique to use for this age group, and it also gets parent(s) or guardian(s) involved with the student's work.

If you want students to use books, software, or the Internet to research careers, the list of jobs found on pages 23–24 might be a good place to start. The jobs listed on these pages represent the jobs at which most people in the United States currently work (85 percent).

Related Reproducible Activity Sheets

The age and type of students you work with and time limits will be, no doubt, the deciding factors for how extensively you pursue career exploration and research. Many of the activities in the reproducible activity sheets relate to career exploration, so you have a variety of activities from which to choose. Thus, you can select those most appropriate for your time frame and students.

- #20—*Career Data Worksheet*
- #21—*Write a Letter to Ask for Career Information*
- #22—*Careers of Famous People*
- #23—*Make a Career Cluster Handbook*
- #24—*Plan a Job Fair*
- #25—*Write a Wild Work Story!*
- #26—*Pick Your "Dream" Career*
- #27—*What's My Line?*
- #28—*Work in Early America*
- #29—*Inventions Create Jobs!*
- #30—*Jobs of the Future*
- #31—*Job Genealogy*
- #32—*Workplaces in Your Community*

Note: The reproducible activity sheets contain a section on "Work and the Needs and Functions of Society," a topic that is not covered *per se* in *Dream Catchers Activities*. If you choose to teach a unit on this topic, you may want to use reproducible activity sheets #28, #29, #30, and #32 at that time rather than now.

Type: In-class or outside of class

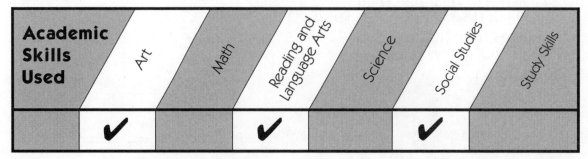

Academic Skills Used	Art	Math	Reading and Language Arts	Science	Social Studies	Study Skills
	✔		✔		✔	

Lesson Plans for Part 1: Capture Your Dreams—The Choice Is Yours

Pages 25-27
Individual activity

Another Kind of Work

Lesson Objective

To introduce students to the concept of volunteer work and its importance.

Activities

Students are first asked to read short stories about volunteers (pages 25-26) and then answer questions to determine how these workers are different from people who get paid to work. They further explore volunteerism by writing about volunteer work they have done.

Students of this age probably have little conception of how much work and the variety of work that is done by volunteers. A good discussion topic might be how much of the work in their school is done by volunteers and what would happen if no one volunteered for those activities. You might want to discuss if volunteer work is the "duty" of all good citizens.

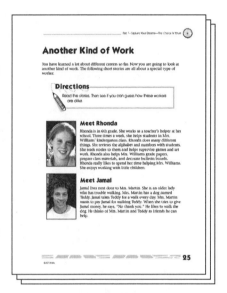

Pages 25-27

Related Reproducible Activity Sheets

- **#33—*Volunteer Work in Your Community.*** This activity allows students to further explore volunteerism through interviewing a person who has done volunteer work.

- **#34—*Plan a Class Volunteer Project.*** This activity suggests that your class plan a volunteer activity of their own. As time permits, you may choose a simple or more involved volunteer project. The activity sheet gives step-by-step instructions for planning a more complex project.

- **#35—*We Need You!—Finding Volunteer Work for Young People.*** Students are asked to find one volunteer program in their community at which people their age could work. After gathering information about the volunteer program, students write a "Want Ad" describing the opportunity.

©JIST Works

Dream Catchers Teacher's Guide

Type: In-class or outside of class

Academic Skills Used	Art	Math	Reading and Language Arts	Science	Social Studies	Study Skills
	✔	✔	✔		✔	

Page 28
Individual activity

Running a Home Is a Big Job!

Lesson Objective

To introduce students to the concept that running a home is a job that involves many skills, a lot of time, and shared responsibility. It also develops an awareness that being a "homemaker" is a job.

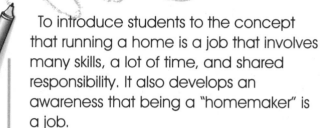

Page 28

Activities

Students are asked to list all the different kinds of jobs that are necessary to keep a household running. Their lists will probably contain many maintenance kinds of jobs such as doing the dishes and laundry. Through class discussion, you might want to have students think about other kinds of work that require more skills, such as balancing a budget, paying bills, sewing, making a fence, fixing a leaky faucet, etc. You might even ask them to think of this kind of work in terms of job titles, such as bookkeeper, plumber, seamstress, groundskeeper, mechanic, and so forth.

You can relate this activity to "The Freedom to Choose" activity (page 18) in terms of stereotyped "women's work" and "men's work" for household activities. Because students are asked to indicate who is responsible for a particular household task, you might compare their answers and see if men and women in their households perform "nontraditional" activities.

Dream Catchers Teacher's Guide

Pages 29–30
Individual activity

Capture Your Dreams

Lesson Objective

To review all concepts introduced in Part 1 of the *Dream Catchers* book.

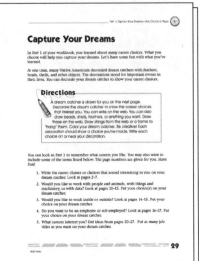
Pages 29–30

Activities

Pages 29 and 30 represent the culminating activity for Part 1. Students are asked to "decorate" the picture of the dream catcher on page 30 to summarize what they have learned and what interests them. They are referred to specific pages in the book to review what has been covered. The same activity is used as the conclusion for Parts 2 and 3.

Note: If your students have made a real dream catcher, you may want them to decorate those instead by hanging "signs" with their choices on them. Another culminating activity is available in the reproducible activity sheets if you prefer not to use the same summarizing activity each time, or you can use both.

Related Reproducible Activity Sheets

- **#36—*Write a Letter Home—Part 1*.** This activity gives students step-by-step instructions for writing a letter home to explain what they have learned in Part 1.

Type: In-class

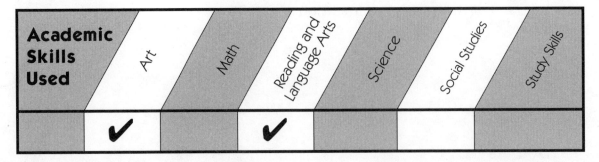

Academic Skills Used	Art	Math	Reading and Language Arts	Science	Social Studies	Study Skills
	✔		✔			

Lesson Plans for Part 2

The Stuff Dreams Are Made Of— Discovering Your Skills

Page 32
Individual activity

What Are Skills?

Lesson Objective

To define the term "skill" and introduce students to the three primary skills important for success at school and at work. To make students aware that they have learned a tremendous number of skills.

Activities

Students are asked to make a list of all the skills they used to get to school today. Although this is a simple activity, it can be used to set a positive tone for this section on skills. If they made a comprehensive list of all the skills they used to get to school, of course it would list hundreds and hundreds of items. Class discussion on this topic can engender a variety of skills and is worth the time to compare student responses and emphasize how much they have learned. The skills they have listed are, of course, self-management skills. You might want to point that out.

This can be an especially important subject for special needs students and students who have low self-esteem. A valuable point to underscore is that just because everyone can do something (e.g., cross a street), it does not lessen the value of the skill. The goal is to encourage students to think of all the things they have learned and can do, so they will feel that they can improve skills in areas that pose difficulties for them.

Lesson Plans for Part 2: The Stuff Dreams Are Made Of—Discovering Your Skills

Page 33
Individual activity

Academic Skills Are Building Blocks

Lesson Objective

To help students understand that their academic skills build upon one another—what they learned previously helps them learn more.

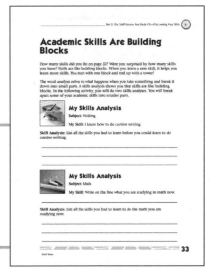

Page 33

Activities

Students are asked to analyze two of their skills by breaking those skills down into "smaller" skills. The first skill is cursive writing; the second is what they are currently working on in math. You may assign that skill for them, e.g., "fractions."

Depending on your class, some students may have difficulty thinking of all the skills they have learned, or they may be too general and "lump" several skills into one. Again, this exercise can build self-esteem and encourage students. It might be worth the time to discuss students' responses and help them make their lists longer, so they can more fully realize what they have achieved already. This might make a good math lesson, especially for students who tend to say, "I don't get it." This activity may help them see that they have understood a great deal already in math, and if they "got" that, they can "get" more.

Related Reproducible Activity Sheets

- #37—*Make a Skills Chain.*
- #38—*Make a Skills Bank.*
- #39—*Share Your Skills.*

These activities are all designed to reinforce the idea that students do have skills and are constantly learning new skills. "Make a Skills Chain" is another method to analyze skills. "Make a Skills Bank" is a continuing activity that positively reinforces the idea that they are always learning and gives students a concrete method to keep track of what they've learned. "Share Your Skills" builds a sense of worth because everyone has a skill they can "teach" or demonstrate to others.

Dream Catchers Teacher's Guide

Type: In-class or outside of class

Academic Skills Used	Art	Math	Reading and Language Arts	Science	Social Studies	Study Skills
	✔	✔	✔			

Lesson Plans for Part 2: The Stuff Dreams Are Made Of—Discovering Your Skills

Page 34
Individual activity

Building a Skills Tower

Pages 35–36
Individual activity

How Strong Is Your Tower?

Lesson Objective

To help students understand that a "weak link" in a skill can affect their overall ability to perform.

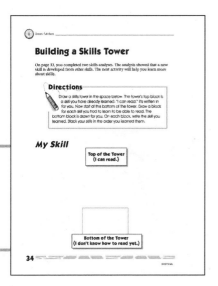

Page 34

Activities

Students perform a skills analysis on their ability to read. They then answer questions directing them to understand how a weakness in one or two skills can affect their ability to read. This activity introduces the concept that to improve in a subject area, they need to identify weaknesses and concentrate on improving them. (Methods to identify specific weaknesses are covered in Part 3.) At this point, establishing the concept of the inter-relatedness of skills is what's important.

A class discussion of their responses to question 4 "Why is it important to learn the new skills you are taught in school?" and question 6 "What have you learned about skills with this activity?" might help them understand the concept that each learned skill is important in building new skills.

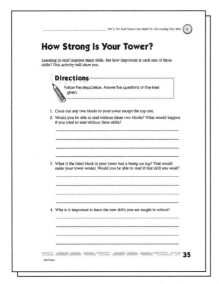

Pages 35–36

©JIST Works

31

Dream Catchers Teacher's Guide

Related Reproducible Activity Sheets

- #40—*You Can Be an Apprentice.*
- #41—*Practice Makes Perfect.*

These activities encourage students to learn new skills and to observe and write about the process of building new skills. Both exercises help students to more fully comprehend the learning process. Activity #40 can be used here, or it can also be used later in Part 2 with the job-related skills section.

Type: Outside of class

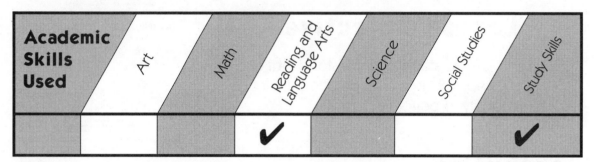

Academic Skills Used	Art	Math	Reading and Language Arts	Science	Social Studies	Study Skills
			✔			✔

Lesson Plans for Part 2: The Stuff Dreams Are Made Of—Discovering Your Skills

Pages 37–39
Individual or class activity

Do Workers Need Academic Skills?

Lesson Objective

To help students understand they will need their academic skills for any career they choose.

Pages 37–39

Activities

Students are asked to read short stories about different workers and identify the academic skills needed for those jobs. This activity can help students see that the work they are doing in school now is important for their future career choices. Its purpose is to demonstrate the connection between schoolwork and the world of work.

If you have your students do reproducible activity sheet #42, class discussion or the small group project listed under "Extra Activity" can help reinforce how many academic skills are used on the job.

Related Reproducible Activity Sheets

- **#42**—*What Academic Skills Are Needed for Jobs?*
- **#43**—*Using Your Academic Skills Outside of School.*

Both activities are designed to help students understand that their academic studies are a preparation for life, not just isolated activities relevant only to the school setting.

Type: In-class or outside of class

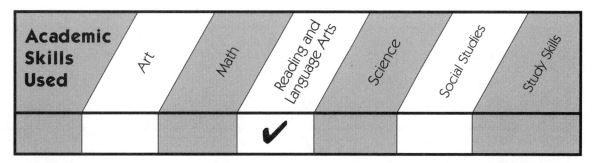

©JIST Works

Dream Catchers Teacher's Guide

Pages 40–41
Individual activity

What Are Self-Management Skills?

Lesson Objective

To help make students aware of the importance of good self-management skills.

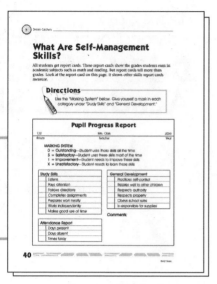

Pages 40–41

Activities

Students are asked to "grade" themselves on self-management skills. A copy of a report card is reproduced for students to use, and it represents the "other things" on a report card besides grades. Most students pay little attention to these marks, yet we know that self-management skills play a large part in the grades students get.

A good discussion here might stem from giving students a copy of the report cards used in your school. Have them discuss the areas on which they are evaluated and see what they think those areas mean. What does it mean, for example, to "practice self-control?" Why is self-control important? What does it mean to "make good use of time?" Why is regular attendance important? (You might relate attendance to building skills too.) After discussion, you might read out loud together the definitions of self-management skills on page 41.

Related Reproducible Activity Sheets

- **#44—*Using Your Self-Management Skills.*** This activity asks students to write about a time when they used good self-management skills. It's a way to demonstrate to students that they can be in control if they choose.

Type: In-class or outside of class

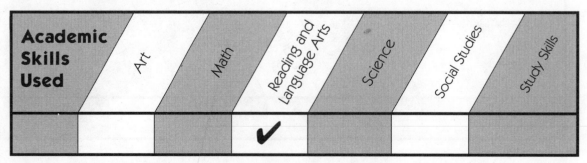

34

©JIST Works

Lesson Plans for Part 2: The Stuff Dreams Are Made Of—Discovering Your Skills

Page 42
Individual activity

My Good Self-Management Skills

Lesson Objective

To help students focus on the self-management capabilities they do have.

Page 42

Activities

This activity asks students to list their good self-management skills. Although the exercise suggests they can begin by looking at the "grades" they gave themselves on the report card, it's important to stress they are not limited to just the school setting. Maybe the student who has difficulties in school is never late for a basketball practice, or always walks the dog, or keeps his or her room clean. The emphasis here is for students to feel positive about some of their self-management accomplishments.

Related Reproducible Activity Sheets

- **#45—*Improving Your Self-Management Skills*.** This activity asks students to think about areas where they need improvement and helps them set goals to improve weak skills.

Type: In-class or outside of class

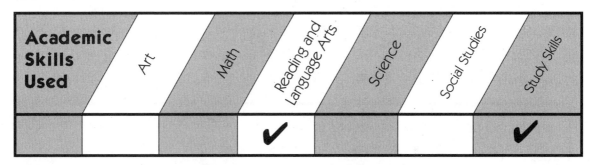

©JIST Works

Dream Catchers Teacher's Guide

Page 43
Individual or small-group activity

Do Employees Get Report Cards?

Lesson Objective

To make students aware that self-management skills are also very important in the world of work.

Activities

Page 43

Students are given a copy of an employee evaluation form and are asked to identify the type of skill on which the employee is being evaluated—academic or self-management. This can be an important concept for students as most of them are probably unaware that workers get evaluated too. In class discussion, you might explain how teachers are evaluated, especially before tenure, and how teachers are expected to continue their education on a regular basis.

You might want to tell them about test taking and licenses that are necessary before people can work at certain occupations. Emphasize how important good self-management skills are to employers.

Related Reproducible Activity Sheets

- #46—*Using Time Efficiently in the Workplace.*
- #47—*Make a School Time Card.* This activity sheet is a class project where timecards are used to keep attendance and track tardiness.
- #48—*The Case of the "Bad Worker."*

Activities #46 and #48 further demonstrate to students the importance of good self-management skills in the workplace.

Type: In-class or outside of class

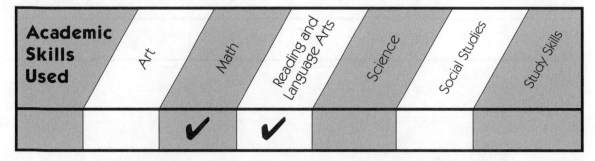

36

©JIST Works

Lesson Plans for Part 2: The Stuff Dreams Are Made Of—Discovering Your Skills

Pages 44–45
Individual or small-group activity

What Are Job-Related Skills?

Lesson Objective

To introduce students to the concept that all jobs require specific skills that must be learned for the worker to do the job.

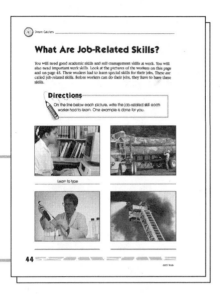

Activities

Pages 44–45

Students are asked to look at pictures of workers and write the job-related skill that worker had to learn to do the work pictured. Answers can be "checked" through small group comparisons or class discussion.

You might want to introduce the idea that some jobs require more skills than others. Ask them to look at the pictures and decide which jobs probably took a longer time to learn or which jobs require more skills than others. As a "warm up" for the next activity, you might ask your students where they think the people pictured learned their job skills and how long it took to learn them.

Related Reproducible Activity Sheets

- #49—*What Job-Related Skills Do You Need?*
- #50—*Create a Job-Related Skills Bulletin Board.*

Both these activities provide further channels to explore the idea of job-related skills.

Type: In-class or outside of class

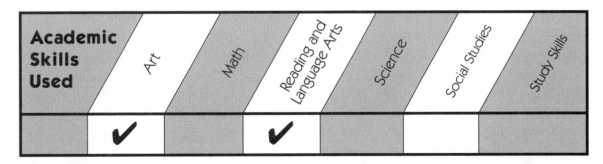

Academic Skills Used	Art	Math	Reading and Language Arts	Science	Social Studies	Study Skills
	✔		✔			

©JIST Works

Dream Catchers Teacher's Guide

Pages 46–47
Individual or small-group activity

Where Can You Learn Job-Related Skills?

Pages 48–49
Individual or small-group activity

Mapping Your Future

Lesson Objective

To introduce students to the variety of education and training options that exist to learn job-related skills.

Pages 46–47

Activities

Students read about a variety of education and training options for learning job-related skills. The text also contains examples of jobs that could be learned there. They are then asked questions about education and training and jobs that are answered by reading the text. Tell students they will have to read the text carefully and probably refer back to it frequently to answer the questions. Answers can be checked in small groups or through class discussion.

People can get training in different ways for the same job, of course. A photographer, for example, could learn through on-the-job-training or in school. You might want to mention that fact, but it probably does not need to be emphasized too much. The point of this exercise is simply to develop awareness that many options for education and training will exist in their futures.

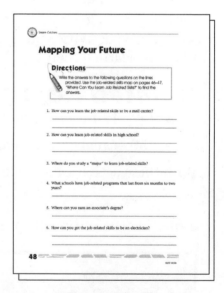

Pages 48–49

©JIST Works

Lesson Plans for Part 2: The Stuff Dreams Are Made Of—Discovering Your Skills

Page 50
Individual or small-group activity

How Is School Like a Job?

Lesson Objective

To review the three types of skills learned in Part 2: academic, self-management, and job-related. To emphasize that these skills are needed for both school and work.

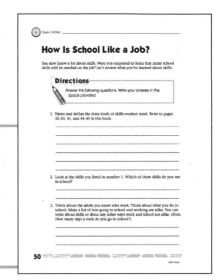

Page 50

Activities

Students answer questions about the kinds of skills they have explored in this part. They also are asked to write their own comparison of school and work. An alternate activity to an individually written piece is to have students make a list of similarities in small groups.

Related Reproducible Activity Sheets

- **#51—*Using the Want Ads to Learn About Skills.*** This is an excellent activity to help students learn about the skills that are required for jobs. Most students are very surprised by the specific skills and behaviors employers are seeking.

Type: In-class

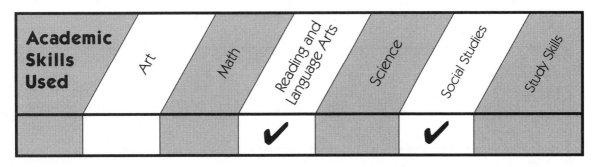

Academic Skills Used	Art	Math	Reading and Language Arts	Science	Social Studies	Study Skills
			✔		✔	

©JIST Works

Dream Catchers Teacher's Guide

Pages 51–52
Individual activity

The Stuff Dreams Are Made Of

Lesson Objective

To review all concepts introduced in Part 2 of the *Dream Catchers* book.

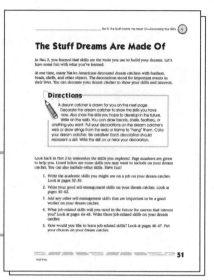

Pages 51–52

Activities

Pages 51 and 52 represent the culminating activity for Part 2. Students are asked to "decorate" the picture of the dream catcher on page 52 to summarize what they have learned and what interests them. They are referred to specific pages in the book to review what has been covered. This same activity is used as the conclusion for Parts 1 and 3.

Note: If your students have made a real dream catcher, you may want them to decorate those instead by hanging "signs" with their choices on them. An alternate culminating activity is available in the reproducible activity sheets if you prefer not to use the same summarizing activity each time. Or you can use both.

Related Reproducible Activity Sheets

- **#52—*Write a Letter Home—Part 2*.** This activity gives students step-by-step instructions for writing a letter home to explain what they have learned in Part 2.

Type: In-class

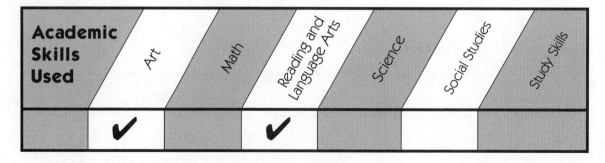

40

©JIST Works

Lesson Plans for   Part **3**

Making Dreams Come True— Ability, Effort, and Achievement

Pages 54–56
Individual or class activity

A Modern Fable of The Three Little Pigs

Lesson Objective

To introduce the roles that ability, effort, and achievement play for success in school and at work.

Pages 54–56

Activities

Trying to discuss the significance of ability, effort, and achievement with students can get, perhaps, a little "heavy" and sound like a sermon. *The Three Little Pigs* tries to get at these concepts through fun with an old nursery story. Although students can read this individually, it's a good story to read out loud to add "dramatic" effects.

Class discussion could center on the moral of the story students are asked to write on their own. You might explain that many fables and popular children's stories were meant to teach lessons to young readers. Ask them if they can think of any stories that were read to them when they were younger that had lessons (*The Little Engine That Could*, for example).

Related Reproducible Activity Sheets

- **#53—*Produce a "Three Little Pigs" Play.*** This activity sheet gives students instructions on how to turn *The Three Little Pigs* into a play. Extra activities include using their stories "Which Little Pig Are You?" as the basis for plays too. Students can present a "Pig Theatre" for another class.

Type: In-class

Academic Skills Used	Art	Math	Reading and Language Arts	Science	Social Studies	Study Skills
	✔		✔			

Page 57
Individual activity

Ability, Effort, and Achievement

Lesson Objective

To allow students to examine their work habits and how they use their abilities in a nonthreatening, nonjudgmental manner.

Activities

Students are asked to pick a pig character from the fable and write a story about a time when they behaved like the pig they selected. All of us at one time or another have been a "Pig I Can," a "Pig I'll Try," or a "Pig I Did It." That's probably a good point to make with your class. This activity can allow them to laugh at some of their shortcomings and, hopefully, in that way avoid a defensive attitude. Emphasize with students that they do not have to select "Pig I Did It," and encourage them to add drama to their stories. These may be good stories to read aloud.

A positive note to end on would be to reiterate the introduction to this activity: They have all been promoted to the grade they're in, which means they have the ability to do the work. You might want to also discuss the parallel between promotions in school and at work.

Pages 58–59
Individual activity

Know Your Strengths ... And Weaknesses

Lesson Objective

To begin to set goals for improving achievement by first identifying strengths and weaknesses.

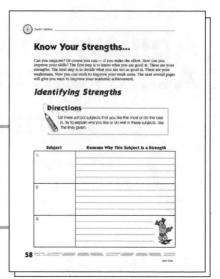

Pages 58–59

Activities

Students have two pages of activities to identify subject areas where they have strengths and weaknesses. They are also asked to identify why this subject is a strength or weakness. Several activities in this part will build on improving study skills and academic achievement; therefore, if students are rather general in their responses at this point, it's OK.

The instructions do ask them to pick subjects that they enjoy the least or do not do well in. Students who generally get good grades can concentrate on subjects they don't like. You might need to make this point in class before they start their analysis.

Lesson Plans for Part 3: Making Dreams Come True—Ability, Effort, and Achievement

Page 60
Individual or small-group activity

Turning a Weakness into a Strength

Lesson Objective

To help students become more specific in their analysis of why a subject might be a weakness.

Activities

Students read a story about Ramon who is having difficulty in math. They are then asked to identify the causes of his problems and offer specific suggestions for improvement. A story format is used first to help students make suggestions more objectively. It's always easier to offer advice to others than follow it yourself!

The story gives several hints as to why Ramon is having difficulty so students need to read it carefully. Their "causes" and "suggestions for improvement" might be good topics for class discussion. Try to guide students to see that specific solutions will be more helpful. Just saying "study more" does not give Ramon a concrete goal that he can measure.

Page 60

Dream Catchers Teacher's Guide

Page 61
Individual activity

You Can Improve, Too!

Lesson Objective

To have students devise a work improvement plan for one of their academic subjects.

Page 61

Activities

This activity asks students to create a work improvement plan for themselves just as they did for Ramon. As before, encourage students to be specific with the methods they select to improve their achievement. You probably should emphasize that their goal is to improve—and that might mean going from a "B" to an "A" or a "C" to a "B." This activity is not just for students who are experiencing serious difficulties.

You might want them to read each other's plans in small groups and compare their solutions. You could put them in groups by the subject area they select. If you think this activity can really help students who are having serious difficulty, you may want to discuss their plans with them.

Related Reproducible Activity Sheets

- **#54—*You Can Improve Too!*** This activity sheet is a reproduction of the activity in the *Dream Catchers* book. It is available here because you might like students to take a copy home to their parent(s) or guardian(s). You might also want them to devise a plan for more than one subject.

Type: In-class or outside of class

Academic Skills Used	Art	Math	Reading and Language Arts	Science	Social Studies	Study Skills
						✓

Lesson Plans for Part 3: Making Dreams Come True—Ability, Effort, and Achievement

Pages 62–63
Individual activity

Managing Your Study Time

Lesson Objective

To help students discover how they use their time.

Pages 62–63

Activities

This activity asks students to keep a journal for one week on how they use their time. Page 63 in *Dream Catchers* provides a sample journal page. At the end of the week, students are then asked to categorize their weekly activities and indicate the time spent on each activity. Page 63 in *Dream Catchers* also provides a sample "Time Spent on My Weekly Activities" chart. Analyzing how they use their time is an important and often revealing exercise for students. Even at a young age, a student's time is frequently heavily scheduled. This exercise develops awareness of the need to manage time, especially to improve academically.

Students may need help categorizing their activities for the "Time Spent on My Weekly Activities" chart when the week is up (another "clustering" activity). You can help them by suggesting broader categories like "play" to include a variety of activities. But make sure they keep watching TV (including movies) and playing video games as separate categories.

At the end of the week, a good discussion topic might be to compare categories and see how much time students are spending on certain activities. Arriving at class totals could be revealing (e.g., how many hours per week as a class do they watch TV as compared to studying?). Students will use this information later on to help establish achievement goals.

Step 1 of the instructions tells students to use notebook paper to create their journal pages. If you have the reproducible activity sheets, a journal page is available there, so you can duplicate pages if you choose. Step 3 tells them to create a chart to record their weekly activities. That chart is available in the reproducible activity sheets too.

Dream Catchers Teacher's Guide

Related Reproducible Activity Sheets

- **#55—*My Time Journal.*** This activity sheet can be used instead of notebook paper when students make their time journal.

- **#56—*Time Spent on My Weekly Activities.*** This activity sheet provides a two-columned chart to categorize and tabulate weekly activities.

- **#57—*How You Use Your Time.*** Making a bar chart of how they use their time is a good method for students to visually compare the time they spend on various activities. A bar chart will have more of an impact than just total numbers.

Type: In-class or outside of class

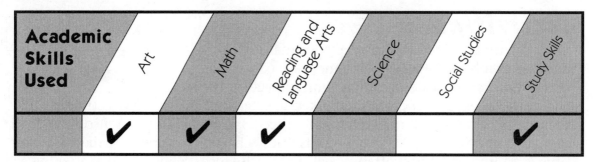

Academic Skills Used	Art	Math	Reading and Language Arts	Science	Social Studies	Study Skills
	✓	✓	✓			✓

Lesson Plans for Part 3: Making Dreams Come True—Ability, Effort, and Achievement

Page 64
Individual activity

A Time-Management Quiz

Lesson Objective

To evaluate how students use their time based on their "Time Journal" findings.

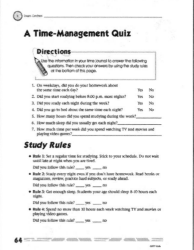

Page 64

Activities

Students are asked to take a quiz to evaluate how they use their study time. Their answers are based on the findings from their time journals. They are then asked to "check" their answers using the "Study Rules" at the bottom of the page.

The class is certain to balk at many of the "rules," like studying even when they don't have assigned homework and limiting TV and video games to no more than 10 hours per week. A class discussion on the "rules" will probably result in a pretty lively debate! Students will use these rules to help set achievement goals later in Part 3.

©JIST Works

Page 65
Individual activity

Organizing Your Workplace at Home

Lesson Objective

To help students realize *where* they study can affect their efficiency.

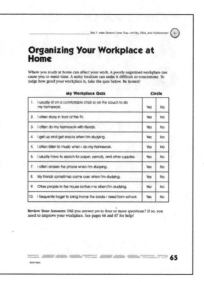

Page 65

Activities

Students are asked to take a "My Workplace Quiz" on their workplace at home. The intent of the quiz is to help them identify study habits that waste time and decrease their efficiency. The key simply says that more than four "Yes" answers means they need to improve. The next activity helps them plan an effective workplace.

Pages 66–67
Individual activity

My Workplace Plan

Lesson Objective

To show students how to make a plan for an efficient study area at home.

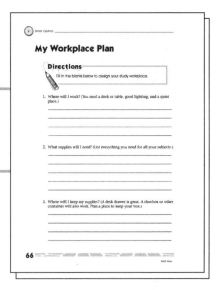

Pages 66–67

Activities

Students are asked to devise a plan for a workplace at home. The plan also includes setting up some study rules.

The plan calls for them to select someplace where they can keep supplies. If your students are not likely to have a desk at home, you might want to make decorating a shoe box or some other box for supplies an in-school activity. Then they could bring it home and enlist the help of an adult to get supplies in it and find a safe storage place.

The workplace plan is reproduced as an activity sheet. Students can take it home to have an adult help them establish a good place to work.

Related Reproducible Activity Sheets

- **#64—*My Workplace Plan*.** This activity is a reproduction of pages 66-67 in the student activity book.

- **#65—*Organizing an Efficient Workplace*.** This activity shows how an efficient workplace is important on the job.

- **#66—*Improving Your School Workplace*.** This activity helps students plan an improved workplace in school, both for personal space (their desks) and the classroom.

- **#67—*Developing a Job Chart*.**

    Activities #66 and #67 encourage students to think of the classroom as their workplace. They offer suggestions on how to organize it, make it more efficient, and have students assume more responsibility for it.

Type: In-class or outside of class

Academic Skills Used	Art	Math	Reading and Language Arts	Science	Social Studies	Study Skills
			✔			✔

Lesson Plans for Part 3: Making Dreams Come True—Ability, Effort, and Achievement

Page 68
Individual activity

Setting Achievement Goals

Lesson Objective

To have students set achievement goals using what they've learned from previous activities.

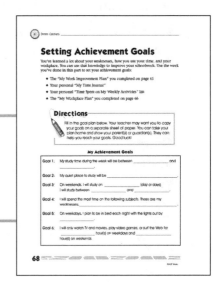

Page 68

Activities

Students will set their goals. (The goal sheet is also available as a reproducible activity sheet, #58, which students can take home.) You might want to add a class project to kick-off their new goal plans. Perhaps the whole class could take a vow to give up TV for a week and use that time reading instead. You can make a "big deal" of this activity by having them sign a pledge and take it home. Their parent(s) or guardians can verify that they didn't watch TV. Rewards could be given to students who keep their pledge.

You might want students to keep a journal in which they indicate whether they have followed their own rules, or devise a method for periodically "checking" themselves. The reproducible activity sheets contain several other worksheets to help students improve study skills. You can use them now or at any time during the year.

Related Reproducible Activity Sheets

- **#58—*Setting Achievement Goals.*** This activity is a reproduction of page 68 in the student activity book.

- **#59—*Make a Schoolwork Planner.*** This activity is a weekly planner that students could use throughout the year.

- **#60—*Managing Your School Study Time.*** This activity applies the same at-home study skills to using study time in school wisely.

- **#61—*Using School Study Time Better.*** This activity applies the same at-home study skills to using study time in school wisely.

- **#62—"*A Test Is Coming!*"** This activity can be used throughout the year to study and review for tests.
- **#63—*Learn from Your Mistakes*.** This activity can be used throughout the year to study and review for tests.

Type: In-class or outside of class

Academic Skills Used	Art	Math	Reading and Language Arts	Science	Social Studies	Study Skills
						✓

Lesson Plans for Part 3: Making Dreams Come True—Ability, Effort, and Achievement

Pages 69–70
Individual activity

Make Dreams Come True

Lesson Objective

To review all concepts introduced in Part 3 of the *Dream Catchers* book.

Pages 69–70

Activities

Pages 69 and 70 represent the culminating activity for Part 3. Students are asked to draw a dream catcher and "decorate" it by summarizing what they have learned and what interests them. They are referred to specific pages in the book to review what has been covered. This same activity is used as the conclusion for Parts 1 and 2.

If your students have made a real dream catcher, you may want them to decorate those instead by hanging "signs" with their choices on them. An alternate culminating activity is available in the reproducible activity sheets if you prefer not to use the same summarizing activity each time—or you can use both.

Related Reproducible Activity Sheets

- **#68—*Write a Letter Home—Part 3*.** This activity gives students step-by-step instructions on writing a letter home to explain what they have learned in Part 3.

Type: In-class

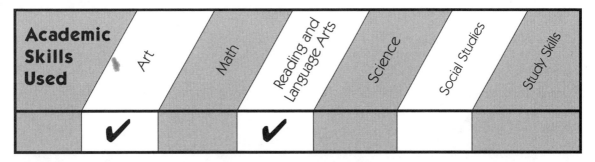

Academic Skills Used	Art	Math	Reading and Language Arts	Science	Social Studies	Study Skills
	✓		✓			

©JIST Works

Lesson Plans for   Part 4

Putting Your Dreams to Work—Work and the Needs and Functions of Society

What You Need to Know About Part 4

Note: This part does not have corresponding pages in the *Dream Catchers* workbook. If you'd like to include this topic in your career awareness unit, you can use the following activities on the next pages.

In addition, the reproducible activity sheets listed below can be *integrated* here rather than in Part 1. Many of these activities ask students to use their social studies book to complete the assignment, so you have the option of integrating this topic into your social studies curriculum, too.

- #28—*Work in Early America*
- #29—*Inventions Create Jobs!*
- #30—*Jobs of the Future*
- #32—*Workplaces in Your Community*

Lesson Plans for Part 4: Putting Your Dreams to Work—Work and the Needs and Functions of Society

Activity Sheet #69

Why Do People Work?

This activity asks students to do a survey on the reasons why people work at the jobs they have chosen. They are instructed to first interview you about the satisfaction you derive from your job and then ask five other adults. As a class, students will compare the results of their survey and see all the different reasons why people work at their jobs.

Class discussion might include the importance of job satisfaction when they choose a career and maybe even any ideas they have now on the subject. Discuss what kind of activities they think will be rewarding.

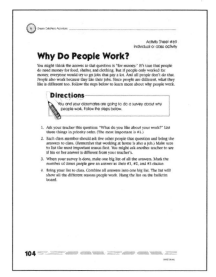

Page 104

Type: In-class and outside of class

Academic Skills Used	Art	Math	Reading and Language Arts	Science	Social Studies	Study Skills
			✓		✓	

Activity Sheet #70

Job Satisfaction— What Do You Want?

In Activity #69, "Why Do People Work?" your class made a list of all the reasons people work. You may have been surprised at the many different reasons given. Besides the need for money, people chose certain careers because they like the work. We call that "job satisfaction." What you do at work makes you feel good or satisfied.

In this activity students are asked to write a report about what kind of job satisfaction they want from a career. They are given four steps to follow.

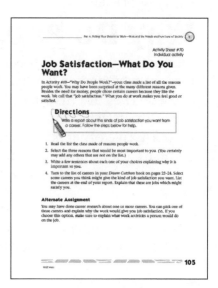

Page 105

As an alternate activity, students can choose one of the careers they researched and explain why the work would give them job satisfaction.

Type: In-class or outside of class

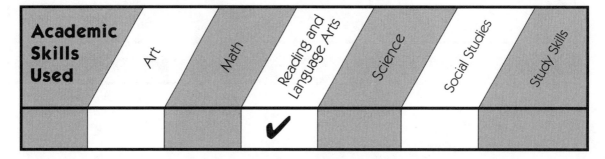

Lesson Plans for Part 4: Putting Your Dreams to Work—Work and the Needs and Functions of Society

Activity Sheet #71

Why Do You Work?

Students are asked to think about the various reasons why they work in school and prioritize them. What satisfaction do they get from schoolwork? They might compare their answers to the answers they received in the adult survey and account for similarities and differences.

Class discussion might center on such topics as why we have laws that say all children have to go to school. Why is having an educated citizenry so important to society that even their parents do not have the right to keep them out of school? Whose needs are being served by sending all children to school?

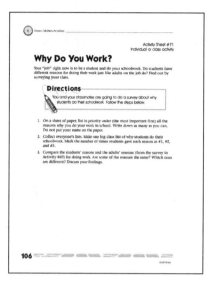

Page 106

Type: In-class or outside of class

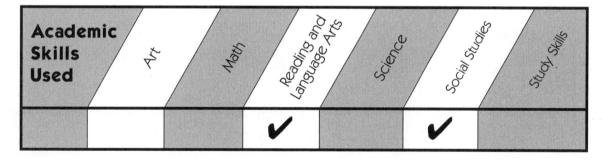

©JIST Works

61

Activity Sheet #72

Work and Society

This activity helps students understand how work done by people in society is interrelated. They are asked to think of all the people and jobs involved in the product cycle of a cotton T-shirt. This activity demonstrates how all workers in the cycle are important for getting the product made. Students make pie charts of all the activities and jobs involved from the beginning of the product until it is purchased by someone.

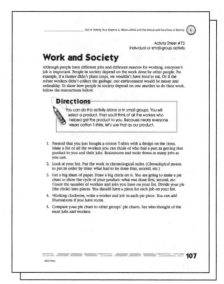

Pages 107-108

This activity works well in small groups. Groups can compare their pie charts and see who thought of the most jobs. Class discussion might examine what would happen if any of the workers in the "pie" decided not to do their work.

Type: In-class

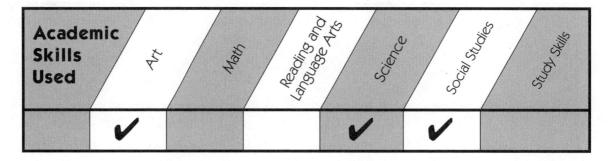

Academic Skills Used	Art	Math	Reading and Language Arts	Science	Social Studies	Study Skills
	✔			✔	✔	

Lesson Plans for Part 4: Putting Your Dreams to Work—Work and the Needs and Functions of Society

Activity #73

Changes in Society and Work

One thing we can always count on is that things change. Our society today is vastly different from what it was like 100 years ago. We all know that. We sometimes don't realize, however, that society changes very quickly, too. Ten years ago, no one had cell phones! Changes in society always affect the world of work. These changes may create the need for new jobs, more workers in a particular job, new products or new business. The needs of society are always reflected in the workforce.

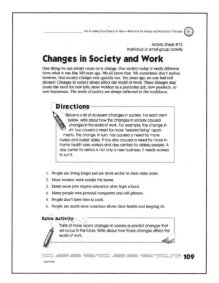

Page 109

In this activity, students are asked to list six recent changes in society and how these changes have affected the world of work.

As an extra activity, students are asked to think of other recent changes in society and predict changes that will occur in the future.

Type: In-class

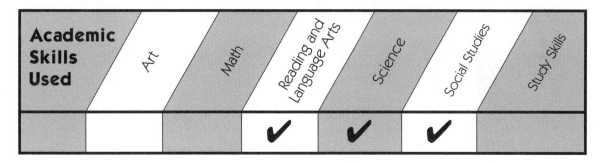

Academic Skills Used	Art	Math	Reading and Language Arts	Science	Social Studies	Study Skills
			✔	✔	✔	

© JIST Works

Activity Sheet #74

The Changing Workforce—Jobs for Robots

In this activity, students are asked to think about personal robots that could do all their chores.

Students are to research the kinds of work robots do. When they finish, they are to write a report about "working robots."

Type: In-class

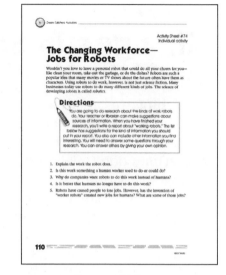

Page 110

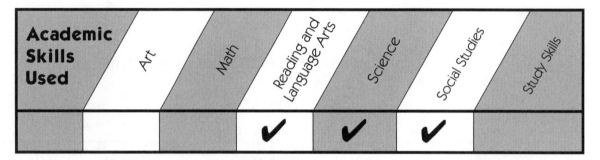

Lesson Plans for Part 4: Putting Your Dreams to Work—Work and the Needs and Functions of Society

Activity Sheet #75

What Would Happen If . . .

This activity also demonstrates how society functions—if people do their work. Students are first asked to list all the different workers in their school. Then they write what the consequences would be if those people did not do their work. Students are asked to decide if the school could function without the workers present and make decisions about which jobs are most vital.

Type: In-class and outside of class

Page 112

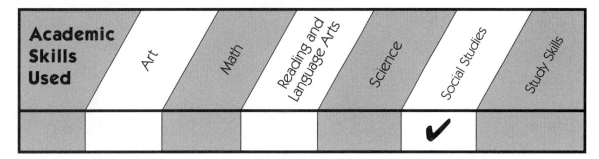

©JIST Works

65

Dream Catchers Teacher's Guide

Activity Sheet #76
On Strike!

This activity explains what a strike is and further explains that in some occupations, it is against the law to strike. Students are asked to think of occupations where if the workers went on strike, the consequences on society would be immediate and extremely serious. They are also asked to guess which occupations are controlled by anti-strike laws.

Type: In-class and outside of class

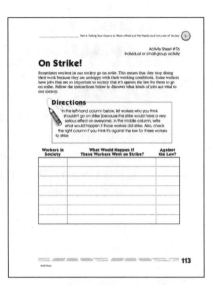

Page 113

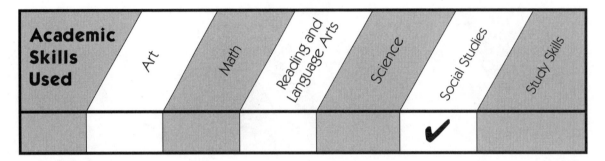

Lesson Plans for Part 4: Putting Your Dreams to Work—Work and the Needs and Functions of Society

Activity Sheet #77

What Are Goods and Services?

This activity introduces students to the concept of goods and services. They are asked to go through the yellow pages of the telephone book and divide the businesses into those that produce goods and those that offer services. The "Extra Activity" section suggests that they can also use the want ad pages to identify jobs in the goods sector and jobs in the services sector.

Depending on how much you want to explore this subject, you can compare percentages of goods and service jobs they find and discuss the fact that service jobs are increasing rapidly in our economy.

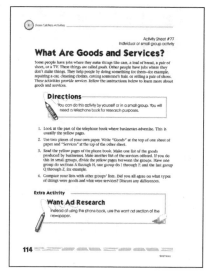

Page 114

Type: In-class and outside of class

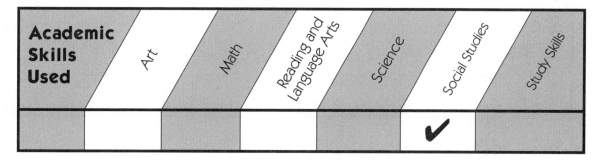

Dream Catchers Teacher's Guide

Activity Sheet #78
Services for Your Home

This activity further develops the idea of providing services as an occupational choice. Students are asked to think of all the things in their houses that might require servicing, or all the jobs they might hire someone to do. They are encouraged to identify the service and the job title of the person who would perform the service.

This would make a good small group competition activity to see which group could come up with the longest list of services and job titles.

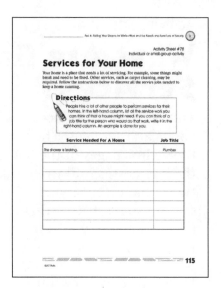

Page 115

Type: In-class and outside of class

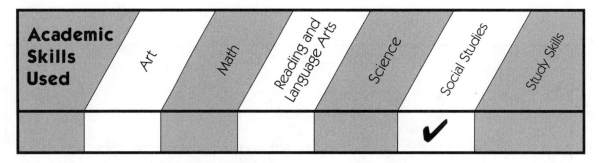

Lesson Plans for Part 4: Putting Your Dreams to Work—Work and the Needs and Functions of Society

Activity Sheet #79

Where Do Goods Come From?

This activity develops the concept of the inter-relatedness of states in producing goods. Students are asked to use their social studies book or an encyclopedia to discover what products or raw materials are produced in certain states. You can assign the state you'd like them to research or have them do several different states by working individually or in small groups.

If students compare research findings, they may be able to make connections between raw materials produced in one state that are used by another state to produce a good. Or you might discuss the products that are used by their families that come from other states.

Page 116

Type: In-class and outside of class

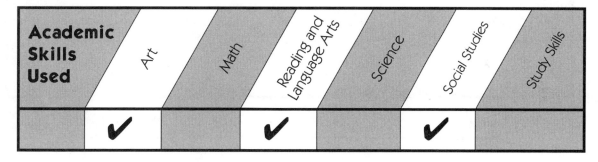

Academic Skills Used	Art	Math	Reading and Language Arts	Science	Social Studies	Study Skills
	✔		✔		✔	

©JIST Works

Activity Sheet #80
The Global Economy

This activity introduces students to the concept of a global economy. It will demonstrate that instead of just an inter-relatedness of states, we are now entering an era of increased inter-relatedness of countries. Students are asked to look at different goods in their homes and bring a list to school of 10 goods and the country where they were produced.

Students then make flags with straight pins and pin their good to a world map. The concrete, visual effect of this activity will help students understand the concept of a global economy. Depending on your students' sophistication, you can discuss what impact a global economy might have on the kinds of jobs that will be available to them in the future.

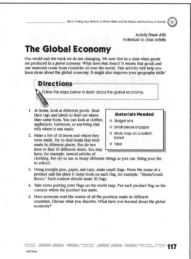

Page 117

Type: In-class and outside of class

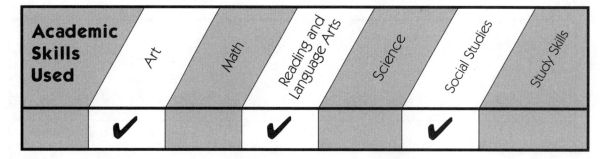

Academic Skills Used	Art	Math	Reading and Language Arts	Science	Social Studies	Study Skills
	✔		✔		✔	

Lesson Plans for Part 4: Putting Your Dreams to Work—Work and the Needs and Functions of Society

Activity Sheet #81

Goods from Around the World

This activity is similar to the activity students performed in discovering the inter-relatedness of states. Instead of states, however, they are asked to use their social studies book or other reference materials to research countries and discover what raw materials and goods they produce. They are further asked to find out if the country they are researching produces goods that we buy in the United States and what other countries buy the goods.

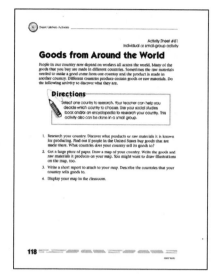

Page 118

Again, you can assign a particular country or have students work in small groups and research several countries.

Type: In-class and outside of class

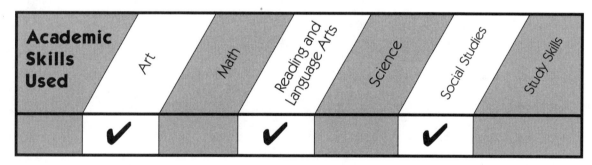

Academic Skills Used	Art	Math	Reading and Language Arts	Science	Social Studies	Study Skills
	✔		✔		✔	

71

©JIST Works

Appendix

Answer Key

Answers to Activities in the Student Workbook

You will not have any difficulty grading the activities in the student workbook. However, the answers to several of the worksheets are provided here to make your job easier. Use them as a reference when reviewing or discussing students' responses.

What Is a Cluster?

Page 2 in the student workbook

Page 9 in this teacher's guide

Following is one answer for each of the clusters. You and your students can think of others. Possible answers are in bold below.

1. Apple, Orange, Banana, Grape, Pear (This one is already filled in for the students.)	Fruit
2. Dog, Cat, Hamster, Goldfish, Bird	Pets
3. Nose, Eye, Ear, Lips, Chin	Things you can see in a small mirror
4. Mom, Dad, Aunt, Brother, Cousin	People you eat with at Thanksgiving
5. Shoes, Jeans, Sweater, Hat, Gloves	Clothes you wear in the fall
6. Bark, Trunk, Leaves, Branches, Roots	Parts of a tree
7. Pronouns, Verbs, Adjectives, Adverbs, Nouns	Parts of speech
8. New York, Miami, Los Angeles, Chicago, Detroit	Cities
9. Ice Cream, Pie, Cake, Cookies, Pudding	Foods you eat after dinner
10. Brush, Paints, Canvas, Easel, Paper	Things an artist uses

Appendix

Find the Right Career Cluster

Pages 8–9 in the student workbook

Pages 10–11 in this teacher's guide

Students are to look at nine pictures of workers and nine career clusters. They are to write the number of the correct career cluster for each picture.

75

©JIST Works

Would You Rather Work Inside or Outside?

Page 15 in the student workbook

Students are given a list of ten careers. They are to determine whether the jobs are done inside or outside. Correct answers are shown in bold below.

1. Mail carrier — **Outside**
2. Data entry worker — **Inside**
3. Airplane pilot — **Inside**
4. Farmer — **Outside**
5. Lawyer — **Inside**
6. Roofer — **Outside**
7. Forest ranger — **Outside**
8. Telephone line repairer — **Outside**
9. Librarian — **Inside**
10. Computer programmer — **Inside**

Who Will You Work For?

Pages 16–17 in the student workbook

Page 19 in this teacher's guide

Students are given the names of ten people and descriptions of what each person does. They are to decide which of the people are employees and which are self-employed. The correct responses are shown in bold below.

1. Sung Lee — **Self-employed**
2. Crystal — **Self-employed**
3. Tavio — **Employee**
4. Robert — **Employee**
5. Jana — **Employee**
6. Duane — **Employee**
7. Nadine — **Self-employed**
8. Maria — **Employee**
9. Dylan — **Employee**
10. Nicole — **Self-employed**

Appendix

Do Workers Need Academic Skills?

Pages 37–39 in the student workbook

Page 33 in this teacher's guide

Students are asked to read the job descriptions of four individuals. They are to identify the academic skills each person uses in his or her job. Correct answers are shown in bold below.

> Page 37 "Surveying the Land," worker's name is Kevin. He needs these academic skills: **Reading, Math, Science, Language Arts, Social Studies.**
>
> Page 38 "Protecting the Lake," worker's name is Lindsay. She needs these academic skills: **Reading, Math, Science, Language Arts, Social Studies.**
>
> Page 38 "Helping Immigrants," worker's name is Andrew. He needs these academic skills: **Reading, Math, Language Arts, Social Studies, Foreign Language.**
>
> Page 39 "Designing Flowers," worker's name is Tanya. She needs these academic skills: **Reading, Math, Language.**

How Is School Like a Job?

Page 50 in the student workbook

Page 39 in this teacher's guide

This activity has three questions. The answers to questions 2 and 3 are subjective, so no answers are given here. In the first question, students are asked to name and define the three kinds of skills workers need. Students should write something similar to the following:

- Academic skills—ones you learn in school
- Self-management skills—good work habits, work attitudes, and interpersonal skills
- Job-related skills—ones you need when doing a certain job

©JIST Works

Notes

Notes

Call 1-800-648-JIST Today!

Dream Catchers, Third Edition

By Norene Lindsay

A complete, ready-to-implement career awareness program for grades 5–9!

- High-interest, flexible career awareness program
- Reinforces the importance of education
- Carefully written to fulfill National Career Development Guidelines

Introduce basic career concepts with this easy-to-use program that includes a student workbook, a teacher's guide, and a book of reproducible worksheet activities. This curriculum is designed to help young people become aware of career options and requirements.

ISBN 1-59357-002-3
Order Code J0023
80 pages
$5.95

- Teaches students to identify their skills
- Introduces basic career concepts
- Develops awareness of the world of work
- Relates school to students' future jobs
- Helps students make plans for improving their academic achievement

Partial Table of Contents

Part 1: Capture Your Dreams—The Choice Is Yours
　　Discovering Career Clusters
　　The Freedom to Choose
　　Career Data Worksheet

Part 2: The Stuff Dreams Are Made Of—Discovering Your Skills
　　Academic Skills Are Building Blocks
　　My Good Self-Management Skills
　　How Is School Like a Job?

Part 3: Make Dreams Come True—Ability, Effort, and Achievement
　　Turning a Weakness into a Strength
　　Managing Your Study Time
　　Organizing Your Workplace at Home

Call 1-800-648-JIST Today!

Dream Catchers Teacher's Guide, Third Edition
By Norene Lindsay

Dream Catchers Teacher's Guide, Third Edition, includes lesson plans for the activities in *Dream Catchers.* Each lesson has a teaching objective and describes activities for individual students, small groups, or the entire class. The teacher's guide includes suggestions for using the reproducible activity sheets from *Dream Catchers Activities.*

- The comprehensive lesson plans reduce your preparation time.
- Pictures of pages from the student workbook are included as a helpful reference for you.
- Each lesson references the corresponding workbook pages and reproducible activity sheets.

The teacher's guide includes Parts 1, 2, and 3, which support the corresponding parts in the student workbook. The teacher's guide also provides a fourth part titled "Putting Your Dreams to Work—Work and the Needs and Functions of Society." This part contains additional lessons you can use to help your students understand the relationship between people's jobs and various aspects of the world of work.

ISBN 1-59357-004-X
Order Code J004X
88 pages
$19.95

What to Look for in Each Lesson

- Activity title
- Workbook page reference
- Suggested teaching format
- Lesson objective
- Picture of the corresponding workbook page
- Activity instructions
- List of related reproducible activity sheets
- Chart showing academic skills used in activity sheets

Call 1-800-648-JIST Today!

Dream Catchers Activities, Third Edition

By Norene Lindsay

Dream Catchers Activities includes over 80 activities for students to complete! If you are using the *Dream Catchers* student workbook as a class text, you can make copies of the pages from *Dream Catchers Activities* for distribution to your class.

Dream Catchers Activities will save you preparation time and serve as a quick, easy reference for you.

All activities are cross-referenced to show the way the activity can be used in the classroom. Activities are included for individual, small-group, or class use.

ISBN 1-59357-003-1
Order Code J0031
128 pages
$24.95

A Sample of Activity Titles

- Careers of Famous People
- Jobs of the Future
- Make a School Time Card
- Using the Want Ads to Learn About Skills
- My Time Journal
- Developing a Job Chart
- Why Do People Work?
- Goods from Around the World